By Laura Williams
Translated by Akosua Boateng

© 2022 Williams Books
1 rue de l'église, 91430 Igny
Dépôt légal : Décembre 2022
ISBN 978-2-494614-19-2
Imprimé à la demande par Amazon
Loi n° 49-956 du 16 juillet 1949 sur les publications destinées à la jeunesse

aprɛ

apple

paya

avocado

kwadu

banana

εdua

beans

kabegyi

cabbage

karɔt

carrot

mako

chilli

aburo

corn

ɛfere

cucumber

ntoropo

eggplant

aanwo

garlic

akakaduro

ginger

aduabunu

green beans

oguaa

guava

ankaatwadeɛ

lemon

amango

mango

mmire

mushroom

gyeene

onion

ankaa

orange

borɔferɛ

papaya

beredum aba

passion fruit

nkateε

peanut

adua nkateɛ

peas

abrɔbɛ

pineapple

abrɔdwoma

potato

ɛfere
pumpkin

εmo

rice

soya

soy

srahansoe

spinach

ahwedeɛ

sugar cane

abrɔdwoma

sweet potato

ntoosi

tomato

anowatere

watermelon

ayuo

wheat

Thank you

Thank you for purchasing "Twi-English Words for Toddlers"! Your support means a lot to me, and I hope you and your child enjoy these books.

If you have a moment, I would greatly appreciate it if you could leave a review on Amazon. Your feedback will help me improve future editions of the series and create more resources for bilingual children.

Thank you again for your support. You can access the reviews on Amazon by scanning the QR code below or by visiting the link below:

https://www.amazon.com/review/create-review?&asin=2494614198

Thank you for helping me continue my work as a language teacher and translator. Your support is greatly appreciated!

In the same collection

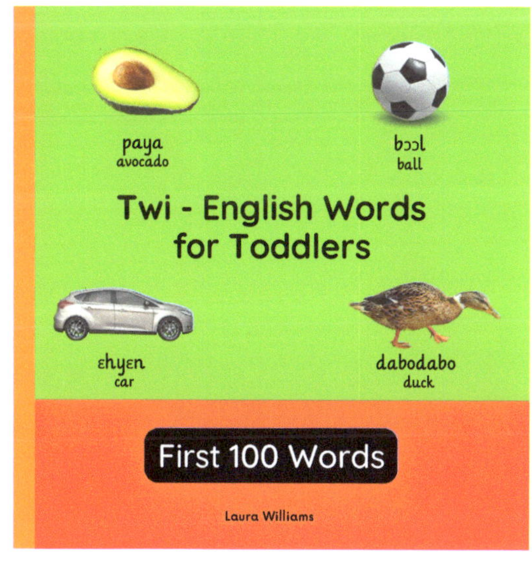

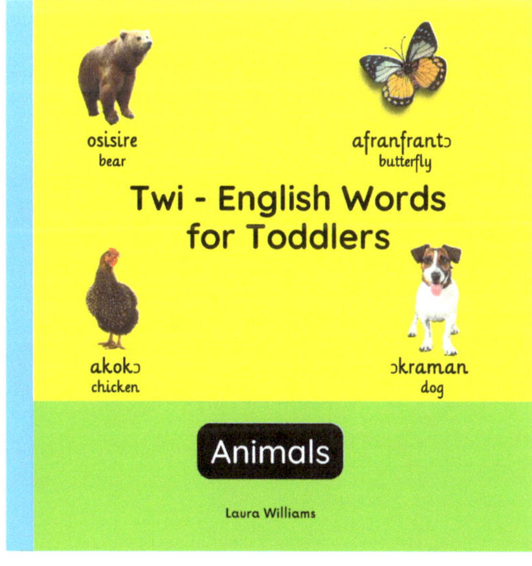